THE WARRIOR ETHOS

STEVEN PRESSFIELD

THE WARRIOR ETHOS

STEVEN PRESSFIELD

Black Irish Entertainment LLC

LOS ANGELES   **NEW YORK**

BLACK IRISH ENTERTAINMENT LLC

65 CENTRAL PARK WEST

NEW YORK, NY 10023

COPYRIGHT © 2011 BY STEVEN PRESSFIELD

BOOK AND COVER DESIGN BY HSU+ASSOCIATES

ART BY BONNIE CLAS

FIRST BLACK IRISH ENTERTAINMENT PAPERBACK EDITION MARCH 2011

FOR INFORMATION ABOUT SPECIAL DISCOUNTS FOR BULK PURCHASES,

PLEASE VISIT WWW.STEVENPRESSFIELD.COM OR WWW.BLACKIRISHENT.COM

ISBN: 978-1-936891-00-9

PRINTED IN THE UNITED STATES OF AMERICA

1 2 3 4 5 6 7 8 9 10

ALSO BY STEVEN PRESSFIELD

FICTION

The Profession

Killing Rommel

The Afghan Campaign

The Virtues of War

Last of the Amazons

Tides of War

Gates of Fire

The Legend of Bagger Vance

NONFICTION

Do the Work

The War of Art

The Spartans do not ask
how many are the enemy
but where are they.

—Plutarch

Sayings of the Spartans

WRITING ABOUT WAR

I am a writer. I write about war—external wars and internal wars, wars ancient and modern, real wars out of history and imagined wars that exist only in speculation. Why? I don't even know myself.

My newest book is called *The Profession*. It's set a generation into the future. *The Profession* posits a world in which combatants, serving for hire, have been cut loose from the traditional rules of war and are no longer bound by the standards of honor that have governed Western armies since Troy and before. This was new territory for me. Questions of right and wrong arose that I had never considered. The subject forced me to do some hard thinking.

Does a fighting man require a flag or a cause to claim a code of honor? Or does a warrior ethos arise spontaneously, called forth by necessity and the needs of the human heart? Is honor coded into our genes? What does honor consist of—in an age when the concept seems almost abandoned by society at large, at least in the West?

What is the Warrior Ethos? Where did it come from? What form does it take today?

This volume is my attempt to address these questions. The book makes no claim to provide an ultimate, definitive answer. It's just one man's thoughts and observations on the subject.

The Warrior Ethos was written for our men and women in uniform, but its utility, I hope, will not be limited to the sphere of literal armed conflict. We all fight wars—in our work, within our families and abroad in the wider world. Each of us struggles every day to define and defend our sense of purpose and integrity, to justify our existence on the planet and to understand, if only within our own hearts, who we are and what we believe in.

We are all warriors. Do we fight by a code? If so, what is it? What is the Warrior Ethos? How do we (and how can we) use it and be true to it in our internal and external lives?

PART ONE

ACADEMIES OF WAR

1

TOUGH MOTHERS

Three stories from ancient Sparta:

A messenger returned to Sparta from a battle. The women clustered around. To one, the messenger said, "Mother, I bring sad news: your son was killed facing the enemy." The mother said, "He is my son." "Your other son is alive and unhurt," said the messenger. "He fled from the enemy." The mother said, "He is not my son."

A different messenger returned from a battle and was hailed by a Spartan mother: "How fares our country, herald?" The messenger burst into tears. "Mother, I pity you," he said. "All five of your sons have been killed facing the enemy." "You fool!" said the woman. "I did not ask of my sons. I asked whether Sparta was victorious!" "Indeed, Mother, our warriors have prevailed."

"Then I am happy," said the mother, and she turned and walked home.

Two warriors, brothers, were fleeing from the enemy back toward the city. Their mother happened to be on the road and saw them running toward her. She lifted her skirts above her waist. "Where do you two think you're running? Back here from whence you came?"

The most famous Spartan mother story is also the shortest:

A Spartan mother handed her son his shield as he prepared to march off to battle. She said, "Come back with this or on it."

That's a warrior culture. That's the Warrior Ethos.

A Spartan colonel, a man in his fifties, was accused of accepting bribes in an overseas command. When his mother back home learned of this, she wrote him the following letter: "Either quit your thieving or quit breathing."

The Warrior Ethos embodies certain virtues—courage, honor, loyalty, integrity, selflessness and others—that most warrior societies believe must be inculcated from birth. In Sparta, every newborn boy was brought before the magistrates to be examined for physical hardiness. If a child was judged unfit, he was taken to a wild gorge on Mount Taygetos, the mountain overlooking the city, and left for the wolves.

We have no reports of a mother weeping or protesting.

2

WOMEN FIRST

One scene in my book *Gates of Fire* has elicited more passionate feedback than any other. It's the one where the Spartan king Leonidas explains what criteria he employed to select the specific 300 warriors that he chose to march off with him and die defending the pass at Thermopylae. The scene is fiction. There's no evidence that anything like it happened in real life. But something about the moment seems to ring so true that it has produced a torrent of letters and e-mails.

Leonidas picked the men he did, he explains, not for their warrior prowess as individuals or collectively. He could as easily have selected 300 others, or twenty groups of 300 others, and they all would have fought bravely and to the death. That was what Spartans were raised to do. Such an act was the apex, to them, of warrior honor.

But the king didn't pick his 300 champions for that quality. He picked them instead, he says, for the courage of their women. He chose these specific warriors for the strength of their wives and mothers to bear up under their loss.

Leonidas knew that to defend Thermopylae was certain death. No force could stand against the overwhelming numbers of the Persian invaders. Leonidas also knew that ultimate victory would be brought about (if indeed it could be brought about) in subsequent battles, fought not by this initial band of defenders but by the united armies of the Greek city-states in the coming months and years.

What would inspire these latter warriors? What would steel their will to resist—and prevent them from offering the tokens of surrender that the Persian king Xerxes demanded of them?

Leonidas knew that the 300 Spartans would die. The bigger question was, How would Sparta herself react to their deaths? If Sparta fell apart, all of Greece would collapse with her. But who would the Spartans themselves look to in the decisive hour? They would look to the women—to the wives and mothers of the fallen.

If these women gave way, if they fell to weeping and despair, then all the women of Sparta would give way too. Sparta herself would buckle and, with her, all of Greece.

But the Spartan women didn't break, and they didn't give

way. The year after Thermopylae, the Greek fleet and army threw back the Persian multitudes at Salamis and Plataea. The West survived then, in no small measure because of her women.

The lioness hunts. The alpha female defends the wolf pack. The Warrior Ethos is not, at bottom, a manifestation only of male aggression or of the masculine will to dominance. Its foundation is society-wide. It rests on the will and resolve of mothers and wives and daughters—and, in no few instances, of female warriors as well—to defend their children, their home soil and the values of their culture.

3

EAST OF EDEN

Where did the Warrior Ethos come from? Why would anyone choose this hard, dangerous life? What could be the philosophy behind such a choice?

An answer may come from the Garden of Eden (which is an archetypal myth common to many cultures other than our own Judeo-Christian).

God sets up Adam and Eve in paradise, where all their needs are met without effort. But He warns them, "Don't go near that tree in the center of the garden." Of course, they do. The mother and father of the human race choose to eat the fruit of the tree of knowledge of good and evil.

In other words, they choose to become human. They acquire a quality of consciousness that, until now, has been the possession of God alone.

God kicks them out—into the land of Nod, east of Eden. And here is the curse He lays upon Adam and Eve (and by extension upon the human race forever):

> Henceforth shalt thou eat thy bread in the
> sweat of thy face.

In other words, from now on you humans have to work for a living.

No more picking fruit for free from the trees. From now on, you have to hunt. You have to chase wild animals and kill them before they kill you.

Adam and Eve became the primitive hunting band. The hunting band became the tribe. And the tribe became the army.

The Warrior Ethos evolved from the primary need of the spear-toting, rock-throwing, animal-skin-wearing hunting band—the need to survive. This need could be met only collectively, as a group working in unison. To bind the band together, an ethos evolved—a hunter's ethos.

Every warrior virtue proceeds from this—courage, selflessness, love of and loyalty to one's comrades, patience, self-command, the will to endure adversity. It all comes from the hunting band's need to survive.

At a deeper level, the Warrior Ethos recognizes that each of us, as well, has enemies inside himself. Vices and weaknesses like envy and greed, laziness, selfishness, the capacity to lie and cheat and do harm to our brothers.

The tenets of the Warrior Ethos, directed inward, inspire us to contend against and defeat those enemies within our own hearts.

4

LORD OF THE BATTLEFIELD

Alexander the Great, toward the end of his life, frequently stayed up all night, sacrificing to the god Fear. Why? Because the ancient way of war was characterized by fear.

The Warrior Ethos evolved as a counterpoise to fear.

In the era before gunpowder, all killing was of necessity done hand to hand. For a Greek or Roman warrior to slay his enemy, he had to get so close that there was an equal chance that the enemy's sword or spear would kill him. This produced an ideal of manly virtue—*andreia*, in Greek—that prized valor and honor as highly as victory.

> Be brave, my heart [wrote the poet and mercenary Archilochus]. Plant your feet and square your shoulders to the enemy. Meet him among the man-killing spears. Hold your ground. In victory, do not brag; in defeat, do not weep.

The ancients resisted innovation in warfare because they feared it would rob the struggle of honor.

> King Agis was shown a new catapult, which could shoot a killing dart 200 yards. When he saw this, he wept. "Alas," he said. "Valor is no more."

The god who ruled the battlefield was Phobos. Fear.

5

THE INSTINCT OF
SELF-PRESERVATION

Some say that self-preservation is the strongest instinct of all, not only in humans but in all animal life. Fear of death. The imperative to survive. Nature has implanted this in all living creatures.

The Warrior Ethos evolved to counter the instinct of self-preservation.

Against this natural impulse to flee from danger (specifically from an armed and organized human enemy), the Warrior Ethos enlists three other equally innate and powerful human impulses:

Shame.

Honor.

And love.

6

RIGHT AND WRONG

The concepts of shame, honor and love imply moral judgment. Right and wrong. Virtues and vices.

The natural, evolution-spawned instinct of self-preservation becomes viewed within the context of an ethical code—and indicted as wrong, evil, cowardly, depraved.

Its opposite—courage—is judged by that same code and declared to be good, brave and honorable.

> The Spartan king Agesilaus was once asked what was the supreme warrior virtue, from which all other virtues derived. He replied, "Contempt for death."

Courage—in particular, stalwartness in the face of death—must be considered the foremost warrior virtue.

> A detachment of Romans was cut off in a waterless place. The enemy commander

13

demanded their surrender. The Romans refused. "You are surrounded," declared the enemy captain in exasperation. "You have neither food nor water. You have no choice but to surrender!" The Roman commander replied, "No choice? Then have you taken away as well the option to die with honor?"

The dictionary defines *ethos* as:

> The moral character, nature, disposition and customs of a people or culture.

Ethos is derived from the same Greek root as *ethics*. The Warrior Ethos is a code of conduct—a conception of right and wrong, of virtues and of vices.

No one is born with the Warrior Ethos, though many of its tenets appear naturally in young men and women of all cultures.

The Warrior Ethos is taught. On the football field in Topeka, in the mountains of the Hindu Kush, on the lion-infested plains of Kenya and Tanzania. Courage is modeled for the youth by fathers and older brothers, by mentors and elders. It is inculcated, in almost all cultures, by a regimen of training and discipline. This discipline frequently culminates in an ordeal of initiation. The Spartan youth receives his shield, the paratrooper is awarded his wings, the Afghan boy is handed his AK-47.

7

TRIBES, GANGS AND TERRORISTS

Every honorable convention has its shadow version, a pseudo or evil-twin manifestation in which noble principles are practiced—but in a "dark side" system that turns means and ends on their heads. The Mafia and criminal gangs live by rigorous and sophisticated codes of loyalty, discipline and honor. So do terrorist organizations. Does that make them warriors? Do these groups practice the Warrior Ethos? When is "honor" not honor?

To answer this, we must consider the nature of tribes. What are the social, cultural and political characteristics of tribes?

First, tribes are hostile to all outsiders. This has been true, anthropologists tell us, of virtually all tribes in all parts of the globe and in all eras of history. Tribes are perpetually at war with other tribes.

Tribes practice the primacy of honor. Tribes are governed not by the rule of law but by a code of honor (*nang*, in

Pashto). Tribal codes mandate the obligation of revenge (*badal*). Any insult to honor must be avenged.

Tribes prize loyalty and cohesion. Tribes revere elders and the gods. Tribes resist change. Tribes suppress women. Tribes value the capacity to endure hardship.

Tribes are patient. Time means nothing in the tribal scheme. Tribes will wait out an invading enemy till he tires and goes home.

> "You've got the watches," say the Taliban,
> "but we've got the time."

Tribes are tied to the land and draw strength from the land. Tribes fight at their best in defense of home soil.

Tribes are adaptable; they will take on any shape or coloration temporarily, if it will help them survive in the long run. Tribes will ally with enemy tribes to repel the greater threat of an invader, then go back to killing one another once the invader has been driven out.

There is much to admire in these qualities. In fact, a strong case could be made that what the U.S. military attempts to do in training its young men and women is to turn them into a tribe. Certainly it's not hard to understand why tribes all over the world make such formidable fighting forces.

But the tribal mind-set possesses two potentially dangerous attributes, which can make its practitioners prey to what we might call "shadow tribalism" or "criminal tribalism," particularly in the modern post- and anti-tribal world.

First, tribes exist for themselves alone. An outsider (unless he falls under the obligation of hospitality) is not considered a human being in the same sense that a tribal member is and is not protected by the same notions of fellow humanity. Tribes are the original us-versus-them social entity.

When this aspect of the honor culture is grafted onto a criminal, political or extremist religious doctrine—read: Mafia, Aryan Brotherhood, al Qaeda—the easy next step is dehumanization and demonization of the enemy.

The Warrior Ethos, on the contrary, mandates respect for the enemy. The foe is granted full honor as a fighting man and defender of his home soil and values. From Cyrus through Alexander to the Greeks and Romans and on down to Rommel and the Afrika Korps (with some notorious lapses, be it said), today's enemy was considered tomorrow's potential friend—and thus granted his full humanity.

Second, tribes are by definition limited in size (since social bonds are usually of blood or kinship) and thus feel vulnerable at all times to bigger or stronger rivals. Tribes live by the siege mentality. They see themselves as surrounded, outnumbered and ever in peril. Again, read: Mob, prison gang, al Qaeda.

The tribal mind–set thus has no trouble embracing the concept of asymmetrical warfare and pushing this to its limits, meaning terrorism and beyond. If the enemy is bigger, stronger and more technologically advanced than we are, says the Mob/gang/terrorist, then we are justified in using any and all methods to strike at him.

Criminal and terrorist organizations practice tribe-like codes of honor, but they do not practice the Warrior Ethos. They are "shadow tribes." They are not warriors. In the practice of terror, in fact, the terrorist organization uses the enemy's embrace of the Warrior Ethos against him. How? By violating the honorable tribal/warrior code in the most shocking and extreme manner—i.e., striking civilian targets, using women and children as human shields, etc.

The terrorist's aim is to so outrage and appall the sense of honor of the enemy that the enemy concludes, "These people are fiends and madmen," and decides either to yield to the terrorist's demands out of fear or to fight the terrorist by sinking to his moral level.

What would Leonidas think of waterboarding or extraordinary rendition? How would Cyrus the Great look upon the practice of suicide bombing or video beheadings on YouTube?

8

THE DIFFERENCE
BETWEEN GUILT AND SHAME

Sociologists tell us that there are two types of cultures: guilt-based and shame-based.

Individuals in a guilt-based culture internalize their society's conceptions of right and wrong. The sinner feels his crime in his guts. He doesn't need anyone to convict him and sentence him; he convicts and sentences himself.

The West is a guilt-based culture. Since the Judeo-Christian God sees and knows our private deeds and innermost thoughts, we are always guilty of something, with no way out save some form of divine absolution, forgiveness or grace.

A shame-based culture is the opposite. In a shame-based culture, "face" is everything. All that matters is what the community believes of us. If we have committed murder but we can convince our fellows that we're innocent, we're home free. On the other hand, if the community believes evil of us—even if we're blameless—we have lost face and honor. Death has become preferable to life.

A shame-based culture imposes its values from outside the individual, by the good or bad opinion of the group. The community imposes its code on its members by such acts as shunning and public shaming.

The Japanese warrior culture of Bushido is shame-based; it compels those it deems cowards or traitors to commit ritual suicide. The tribal cultures of Pashtunistan are shame-based. The Marine Corps is shame-based. So were the Romans, Alexander's Macedonians and the ancient Spartans.

> The maidens of Sparta were taught songs of ridicule with which to humiliate any young man who displayed want of courage in battle. When a warrior accused of being a "trembler" returned to the city, the pretty young girls clustered around him, mocking him and defaming him with these anthems of shame.

Remember the Spartan mother who lifted her skirts to chastise her sons: "Where are you running—back here from whence you came?"

If a Spartan youth failed to show courage in battle, his fiancée would abandon him. The magistrates would not permit him to marry or, if he was married already, he and his wife were forbidden to have children. If the warrior had sisters of marriageable age, their suitors would be compelled to part from them. The man's whole family would be shunned.

> At Thermopylae in 480 B.C., every one of the 300 Spartans died resisting the Persian invaders except one, a warrior named Aristodemus who was withdrawn at the last minute because an eye inflammation had rendered him temporarily blind. The next year, the Spartans again faced the Persians, at Plataea, in central Greece. This time, Aristodemus was healthy and fought in the front rank. When the battle was over, all who had witnessed his actions agreed that Aristodemus had earned the prize of valor, so brilliant and relentless had been his courage. But the magistrates refused to award him this honor, judging that he was driven by such shame that he risked his life recklessly,

deliberately seeking to die.

9

THE OPPOSITE OF SHAME
IS HONOR

Once, in India, after years on campaign, Alexander's men threatened to mutiny. They were worn out and wanted to go home. Alexander called an assembly. When the army had gathered, the young king stepped forth and stripped naked.

> "These scars on my body," Alexander declared, "were got for you, my brothers. Every wound, as you see, is in the front. Let that man stand forth from your ranks who has bled more than I, or endured more than I for your sake. Show him to me, and I will yield to your weariness and go home." Not a man came forward. Instead, a great cheer arose from the army. The men begged their king to forgive them for their want of spirit and pleaded with him only to lead them forward.

By challenging them to show more scars on their bodies than he had on his, Alexander was shaming his men. Warrior cultures (and warrior leaders) enlist shame, not only as a counter to fear but as a goad to honor. The warrior advancing into battle (or simply resolving to keep up the fight) is more afraid of disgrace in the eyes of his brothers than he is of the spears and lances of the enemy.

10

BOYZ 2 MEN

When they were boys, Alexander and his friends were forced to bathe in frigid rivers, run barefoot till their soles grew as thick as leather, ride all day without food or water and endure whippings and ritual humiliations. On the rare occasions when they got to rest, their trainers would remind them, "While you lie here at ease, the sons of the Persians are training to defeat you in battle."

In Sparta, boys were allowed to stay with their mothers till they were seven. At that age, they were taken from their families and enrolled in the *agoge*, "the Upbringing." This training lasted till they were eighteen, when they were considered grown warriors and were enrolled in the army.

> The boys in training were given one garment, a rough cloak that they wore all year long. They slept out of doors year-round. Each boy carried a sickle-like weapon called a *xyele*. They were allowed no beds but instead had to

make nests of reeds gathered each night from the river. They were not permitted to cut the reeds with their sickles but had to tear them with their bare hands.

Food for the boys was pig's-blood porridge. A visiting Persian envoy was once given a taste of this gruel:

> Now I understand Spartan courage in battle. For surely death is preferable to dining upon such slop.

Bad as the food was, the boys got little of it. Instead, they were encouraged to steal. Stealing was no crime, but getting caught was. A boy who got caught was whipped. To cry out was considered a sign of cowardice. It was not unheard of for a Spartan boy to die of a beating without uttering a sound.

> In my day [said the first-century historian Plutarch], tourists traveled hundreds of miles to witness these scourgings, and to behold the courage of the boys enduring them in silence.

There was a footrace in Sparta each year among the boys. They ran ten miles, barefoot, carrying a mouthful of water. The boys were not allowed to swallow any of the water but had to spit it all out at the end of the race.

Spartan boys were not permitted to speak to their elders unless spoken to. When addressed by their seniors, they stood in their rough cloaks, hands respectfully inside the garment, with their eyes on the ground.

> Once a Spartan boy stole a fox and hid it under his cloak. Some grown warriors stopped to question him on an unrelated subject. Beneath the cloak, the fox began gnawing at the youth's belly. The boy made no sound but allowed the beast to bleed him to death, rather than cry out or reveal his deed.

STEVEN PRESSFIELD

PART TWO

THE EXTERNAL WAR

11

RUGGED LAND

Many warrior cultures have arisen in harsh physical environments. Greeks and Macedonians; Romans and Russians; even the British and Japanese, isolated on their resource-poor islands; as well as the Masai and the Apache; the Zulu and the Bedouin; the clansmen of the Scottish Highlands; in Afghanistan, the Pashtun tribesmen of the Hindu Kush. Here in America, the mountain and hill country of Virginia and West Virginia, Kentucky, Tennessee and southern Missouri (not to mention the Carolinas, Georgia and Texas) has produced outstanding soldiers from the Civil War to the present.

The interesting thing about peoples and cultures from rugged environments is that they almost never choose to leave them. When the Persians under Cyrus the Great (who came from the harsh Zagros Mountains, in what is today Iran) conquered the lowland Medes 2700 years ago, the royal advisors assumed that Cyrus would abandon his barren, rocky homeland and settle in to the good life in the Medes' fertile valleys. But Cyrus knew, as the proverb declares, that "soft lands make soft people." His answer became famous throughout the world:

> Better to live in a rugged land and rule than
> to cultivate rich plains and be a slave.

When Alexander invaded Afghanistan in the 330s B.C., he allied himself with numerous tribes and set about making their lives better and easier by building roads into their mountain valleys, so that they could trade and prosper. Emerging from winter quarters the following year, Alexander found all the roads destroyed. The tribes he had built them for had done it. They didn't want trade or prosperity; they preferred isolation and freedom.

The idea of a rugged land can be applied psychologically as well.

There's a well-known gunnery sergeant in the Marine Corps who explains to his young Marines, when they complain about pay, that they get two kinds of salary—a financial salary and a psychological salary. The financial salary is indeed meager. But the psychological salary? Pride, honor, integrity, the chance to be part of a corps with a history of service, valor, glory; to have friends who would sacrifice their lives for you, as you would for them—and to know that you remain a part of this brotherhood as long as you live. How much is that worth?

12

HOW THE SPARTANS
BECAME THE SPARTANS

All warrior cultures start with a great man.

In ancient Sparta, that man was Lycurgus. He took the city from a normal society to a warrior culture.

> So that no man would have grounds to feel superior to another, Lycurgus divided the country into 9000 equal plots of land. To each family, he gave one plot. Further, he decreed that the men no longer be called "citizens" but "peers" or "equals."

> So that no man might compete with another or put on airs over wealth, Lycurgus outlawed money. A coin sufficient to purchase a loaf of bread was made of iron, the size of a man's head and weighing over thirty pounds. So ridiculous was such coinage that men no longer coveted wealth but pursued virtue instead.

Lycurgus outlawed all occupations except warrior. He decreed that no name could be inscribed on a tombstone except that of a woman who died in childbirth or a man killed on the battlefield. A Spartan entered the army at eighteen and remained in service till he was sixty; he regarded all other occupations as unfitting for a man.

> Once, a Spartan was visiting Athens. His Athenian host threw a banquet in his honor. Wishing to show off for his guest, the Athenian indicated several illustrious personages around the table. "That man there is the greatest sculptor in Greece," he declared, "and that gentleman yonder is its finest architect." The Spartan indicated a servant from his own entourage. "Yes," he said, "and that man there makes a very tasty bowl of soup."

The Athenians, of course, were outstanding warriors in their own right. The great playwright Aeschylus, composing his own epitaph, mentioned nothing of his ninety plays or of any other civilian accomplishment.

Here lies Aeschylus the Athenian. Of his courage at the battle of Marathon, the long-haired Persian could speak much.

Lycurgus decreed that no man under thirty could eat dinner at home with his family. Instead, he instituted "common messes" of fourteen or fifteen men who were part of the same platoon or military unit. Above the threshold of each mess was a sign that said:

Out this door, nothing.

The point of the common mess was to bind the men together as friends. "Even horses and dogs who are fed together," observed Xenophon, "form bonds and become attached to one another."

The payoff came, of course, on the battlefield.

Here's how Spartans got married. Lycurgus wanted to encourage passion, because he felt that a child—a boy— conceived in heat would make a better warrior. So a young Spartan husband could not live with his bride (he spent all day training and slept in the common mess). If the young couple were to consummate their love, the husband had to sneak away from his messmates, then slip back before his absence was discovered.

It was not uncommon for a young husband to be married for four or five years and never see his bride in daylight, except during public events and religious festivals.

13

THE OPPOSITE OF FEAR IS LOVE

The greatest counterpoise to fear, the ancients believed, is love—the love of the individual warrior for his brothers in arms. At Thermopylae on the final morning, when the last surviving Spartans knew they were all going to die, they turned to one of their leaders, the warrior Dienekes, and asked him what thoughts they should hold in their minds in this final hour to keep their courage strong. Dienekes instructed his comrades to fight not in the name of such lofty concepts as patriotism, honor, duty or glory. Don't even fight, he said, to protect your family or your home.

> Fight for this alone: the man who stands at your shoulder. He is everything, and everything is contained within him.

The soldier's prayer today on the eve of battle remains not "Lord, spare me" but "Lord, let me not prove unworthy of my brothers."

Civilians wonder at the passion displayed by wounded soldiers to get back to their units, to return to the fight. But soldiers understand. It is no marvel to them that men who have lost arms and legs still consider themselves fit for battle, so powerful is the passion to return to their brothers—and not to let them down.

All warrior cultures train their youths to feel this love. They make the young men on the passage to warriorhood dress alike, eat and sleep alike, speak alike, wear their hair alike, suffer alike and achieve victory alike.

Ordeals of initiation are undergone not as individuals but as teams, as units.

Courage is inseparable from love and leads to what may arguably be the noblest of all warrior virtues: selflessness.

14

SELFLESSNESS

Plutarch asked, "Why do the Spartans punish with a fine the warrior who loses his helmet or spear but punish with death the warrior who loses his shield?"

> Because helmet and spear are carried for the protection of the individual alone, but the shield protects every man in the line.

The group comes before the individual. This tenet is central to the Warrior Ethos.

Once, Alexander was leading his army through a waterless desert. The column was strung out for miles, with men and horses suffering terribly from thirst.

> Suddenly, a detachment of scouts came galloping back to the king. They had found a small spring and had managed to fill up a helmet with water. They rushed to Alexander and presented this to him. The army held in

place, watching. Every man's eye was fixed upon his commander. Alexander thanked his scouts for bringing him this gift, then, without touching a drop, he lifted the helmet and poured the precious liquid into the sand. At once, a great cheer ascended, rolling like thunder from one end of the column to the other. A man was heard to say, "With a king like this to lead us, no force on earth can stand against us."

There's another story of Alexander. When he was getting ready to march out from Macedonia to commence his assault on the Persian Empire, he called the entire army together, officers and men, for a great festival at a place called Dium on the Magnesian coast.

When all the army had assembled, Alexander began giving away everything he owned. To his generals he gave great country estates (all properties of the crown); he gave timberlands to his colonels, fishing grounds, mining concessions and hunting preserves to his midrank officers. Every sergeant got a farm; even privates received cottages and pasturelands and cattle. By the climax of this extraordinary evening, his soldiers were begging their king to stop. "What," one of his friends asked, "will you keep for yourself?" "My hopes," said Alexander.

Selflessness produces courage because it binds men together and proves to each individual that he is not alone. The act of openhandedness evokes desire in the recipient to give back. Alexander's men knew, from their king's spectacular gestures of generosity, that the spoils of any victory they won would be shared with them too, and that their young commander would not hoard the bounty himself. We, in our day, know from history that this was no calculated gesture or grandstanding stunt on Alexander's part. It sprung from the most authentic passions of his heart. He truly cared nothing for material things; he loved his men, and his heart was set on glory and the achievement of great things.

Another time, Alexander's army was struggling through the mountains in the dead of winter. One old soldier came straggling into camp, so frozen from the blizzard that he could no longer see or hear.

Troops around the fire cleared a seat for the veteran, prepared hot broth for him and helped thaw him out. When the ancient soldier had recovered enough to comprehend his surroundings, he realized that the young warrior who had given him his seat by the fire was Alexander himself. At once, the veteran leapt to his feet, apologizing for taking the king's place. "No, my friend," said Alexander, setting a hand on the man's shoulder and making him sit again. "For you are Alexander, more even than I."

15

CITATIONS FOR VALOR

Decorations for valor, from ancient days to modern, have seldom been awarded for raw bloodthirstiness or the brute act of producing carnage. The feat that inspires witnesses to honor it is almost invariably one of selflessness. The hero (though virtually no recipient chooses to call himself by that name) often acts as much to preserve his comrades as he does to deliver destruction onto the foe.

In citations, we read these phrases again and again:

"Disregarding his own safety . . ."

"With no thought for his own life . . ."

"Though wounded numerous times and in desperate need of care for himself . . ."

Selflessness. The group comes before the individual.

16

"FOLLOW ME!"

During the Six Day War, the Yom Kippur War and all of Israel's subsequent conflicts, casualties sustained by officers have exceeded proportionally by far those suffered by men of the enlisted ranks. Why? Because the primary leadership principle that Israeli officers are taught is "Follow me."

> During the Sinai Campaign of 1956, the commander of an Israeli armored regiment violated orders and attacked down the length of the Mitla Pass, sacrificing numerous men and vehicles to capture a strongpoint that was later given up. Despite public outrage at this act of insubordination, the Israeli commander-in-chief, General Moshe Dayan, refused to discipline the man. "I will never punish an officer for daring too much, but only too little."

In the historic clashes of the Granicus River, Issus and Gaugamela, Alexander the Great's order of battle ran like this: allied horse on the left, infantry phalanx in the center, "Silver Shields" to their right, then the elite Companion Cavalry. At the head of this 1600-man detachment rode Alexander himself, on his warhorse, Bucephalus, wearing a double-plumed helmet that could be seen by every man in the army. He led the charge in person and prided himself on being first to strike the enemy.

This is the concept of leading by example. But it also embodies the ancient precept that killing the enemy is not honorable unless the warrior places himself equally in harm's way— and gives the enemy an equal chance to kill him.

The samurai code of Bushido forbade the warrior from approaching an enemy by stealth. Honor commanded that he show himself plainly and permit the foe a fighting chance to defend himself.

During the North Africa campaign of 1940–42, Field Marshal Erwin Rommel led from so far forward that, three times, he either drove or flew himself smack among the British enemy and escaped only by blind luck and wild daring. Rommel's aggressiveness was matched by his sense of fair play and honor.

A company of the Afrika Korps had surrounded a British artillery battery and was demanding its surrender. The German captain had captured an English officer named Desmond Young; with a gun in his hand, the captain commanded Young to order his men to give themselves up. Young refused. At this moment, Rommel chanced to come upon the scene in his staff car. The captain explained the situation, certain that Rommel, his commanding general, would back him up. Instead, the Desert Fox ordered the captain to put away his weapon and to cease demanding of his British prisoner that he order his own men to surrender. "Such an act," Rommel said, "runs counter to the honorable conventions of war." He ordered his captain to find some other solution, while he himself took the Englishman Young aside and shared with him cool water and tea from his own canteen.

Desmond Young, a few years later, authored *Rommel the Desert Fox*, the first great biography of the Afrika Korps commander.

17

THE JOYS OF MISERY

Among all elite U.S. forces, the Marine Corps is unique in that its standards for strength, athleticism and physical hardiness are not exceptional. What separates Marines, instead, is their capacity to endure adversity. Marines take a perverse pride in having colder chow, crappier equipment and higher casualty rates than any other service. This notion goes back to Belleau Wood and earlier, but it came into its own during the exceptionally bloody and punishing battles at Tarawa and Iwo Jima, the Chosin Reservoir and Khe Sanh. Marines take pride in enduring hell. Nothing infuriates Marines more than to learn that some particularly nasty and dangerous assignment has been given to the Army instead of to them. It offends their sense of honor.

This is another key element of the Warrior Ethos: the willing and eager embracing of adversity.

In 1912, the Antarctic explorer Ernest Shackleton was seeking volunteers for an expedition to the South Pole. He placed the following ad in the *London Times:*

> Men wanted for hazardous journey, small wages,
> bitter cold, long months of complete darkness,
> constant danger, safe return doubtful; honor
> and recognition in case of success.

The next morning, 5000 men lined up to volunteer.

The payoff for a life of adversity is freedom. There's a story of the tribes in ancient Afghanistan. When Alexander was preparing to invade the Wild Lands of the Scythians in 333 B.C., a tribal delegation came to him and warned him, for his own good, to stay away. In the end—the Scyths told Alexander—you and your army will come to grief, as all other invaders have in the past (including our friend Cyrus the Great, who was killed north of Mazar-i-Sharif and whose body was never recovered).

> "You may defeat us," said the tribal elders,
> "but you will never defeat our poverty."

What the Scythians meant was that they could endure greater adversity even than Alexander and his Macedonians.

> When the Spartans and their allies overcame
> the Persians at Plataea in 479 B.C., the spoils

included the great pavilion tents of King Xerxes, along with the king's cooks, wine stewards and kitchen servants. For a joke, the Spartan king Pausanias ordered the Persian chefs to prepare a typical dinner, the kind they would make for the Persian king. Meanwhile, he had his own cooks whip up a standard Spartan meal.

The Persian chefs produced a lavish banquet composed of multiple courses, served on golden plates and topped off by the most sumptuous cakes and delicacies. The Spartans' grub was barley bread and pig's-blood stew. When the Spartans saw the two meals side by side, they burst out laughing. "How far the Persians have traveled," declared Pausanias, "to rob us of our poverty!"

18

DUTY, HONOR, COUNTRY

If shame is the negative, honor is the positive. *Nang* in Pashto is honor; *nangwali* is the code of honor by which the Pashtun tribal warrior lives. Bushido is the samurai code. Every tattoo parlor adjacent to a U.S. Marine base has this in innumerable design variations:

Death Before Dishonor

In warrior cultures—from the Sioux and the Comanche to the Zulu and the mountain Pashtun—honor is a man's most prized possession. Without it, life is not worth living.

In 413 B.C., the Spartans sent a general named Gylippus to help their Sicilian allies in the city of Syracuse, which was under siege by the Athenians. Gylippus's first job was to pick from the civilian population those men who would make the best military officers. Gylippus instructed his lieutenants to seek neither men who craved wealth nor those who sought power, but to select only those who desired honor.

Honor, under tribal codes, is a collective imperative. If a man receives an insult to his honor, the offense is felt by all the males in his family. All are mutually bound to avenge the affront.

The American brand of honor is inculcated on the football field, in the locker room and in the street. Back down to no one, avenge every insult, never show fear, never display weakness. Play hurt, never quit.

At Thermopylae in 480 B.C., the Persian king Xerxes, at the head of an army of 2 million men, demanded of the Spartan king Leonidas that he and his 4000 defenders lay down their arms. Leonidas responded in two words: *"Molon labe."*

"Come and take them."

If you travel to Thermopylae today, you'll see the Leonidas monument. It has only two words on it.

The American brigadier general Anthony McAuliffe went

Leonidas one better. Surrounded by the Germans at Bastogne in World War II, the commander of the 101st Airborne replied to the enemy's demand to surrender with one word:

Nuts.

Warrior cultures employ honor, along with shame, to produce courage and resolve in the hearts of their young men.

Honor is the psychological salary of any elite unit. Pride is the possession of honor.

Honor is connected to many things, but one thing it's not connected to is happiness. In honor cultures, happiness as we think of it—"life, liberty and the pursuit of happiness"—is not a recognized good. Happiness in honor cultures is the possession of unsullied honor. Everything else is secondary.

In the West, pride and honor are anachronistic these days. The practitioners of honor are often ridiculed in popular culture, like Jack Nicholson's Marine colonel in *A Few Good Men:* "You can't handle the truth!" Or Robert Duvall in *Apocalypse Now:* "I love the smell of napalm in the morning."

19

THE WILL TO VICTORY

When Alexander was a boy, a party of traders came to Pella, the Macedonian capital, selling trained warhorses. Philip the king and all his officers went down to the plain to put these mounts through their paces. One horse, called Bucephalus, was by far the fastest, strongest and bravest—but he was so wild that no one could ride him. Alexander watched as his father let the steed go without making an offer. "What a fine mount you lose, Father," he said, "for want of spirit to ride him." At this, the king and all his officers laughed. "And what will you pay for this horse, my son—if you can ride him?" "All of my prince's inheritance." So they let the boy try.

Now, Alexander had noticed something about the horse that no one else had—that the beast was spooked by its own shadow.

So he took Bucephalus's bridle and turned him to face into the sun. Then, little by little, speaking gently to him and stroking his neck, he succeeded in quieting the steed down; next, with a quick leap, he sprung onto the horse's back. Philip and the officers watched in breathless trepidation as the prince took this fiery mount out onto the track and spurred him to the gallop. Would the horse throw Alexander, trample him or break his neck? Alexander coolly brought the animal under control and raced him full tilt around the circuit. When he returned to the grandstand, the officers cheered him wildly, while Philip came forward with tears in his eyes and took his son into his arms. "Look you for a kingdom far greater than ours, my son. For Macedonia is plainly too small for you!"

Patton said, "Americans play to win at all times. I wouldn't give a hoot in hell for a man who lost and laughed. That's why Americans have never lost a war and never will lose one."

The will to fight, the passion to be great, is an indispensable element of the Warrior Ethos. It is also a primary quality of leadership, because it inspires men and fires their hearts with ambition and the passion to go beyond their own limits.

Epaminondas, the great Theban general, was the first to beat the Spartans—at the battle of Leuctra in 371 B.C.

> The evening before the fight, Epaminondas called his warriors together and declared that he could guarantee victory on the morrow if his men would vow to perform one feat *at the moment he commanded it.* The men, of course, responded aye. "What do you wish us to do?" "When I sound the trumpet," said Epaminondas, "I want you to give me one more foot. Do you understand? Push the enemy back just one foot." The men swore they would do this.
>
> Battle came. The armies clashed and locked up, shield against shield, each side straining to overcome the other. Epaminondas watched and

waited till he judged both armies had reached the extremity of exhaustion. Then he ordered the trumpet sounded. The warriors of Thebes, remembering their promise, summoned their final reserves of strength and pushed the foe back only one foot. This was enough. The Spartan line broke. A rout ensued.

The will to victory may be demonstrated in places other than actual battle.

A Roman general was leading his legions toward the enemy in a swampy country. He knew that the next day's battle would be fought on a certain plain because it was the only dry, flat place for miles. He pushed his army all night, marching them through a frightening and formidable swamp, so that they reached the battle site before the foe and could claim the high ground. In the aftermath of victory, the general called his troops together and asked them, "Brothers, when did we win the battle?" One captain replied, "Sir, when the infantry attacked." Another said, "Sir, we

59

won when the cavalry broke through." "No," said the general. "We won the battle the night before—when our men marched through that swamp and took the high ground."

20

DIE LAUGHING

The warrior sense of humor is terse, dry—and dark. Its purpose is to deflect fear and to reinforce unity and cohesion.

The Warrior Ethos dictates that the soldier make a joke of pain and laugh at adversity. Here is Leonidas on the final morning at Thermopylae:

> "Now eat a good breakfast, men. For we'll all
> be sharing dinner in hell."

Spartans liked to keep things short. Once, one of their generals captured a city. His dispatch home said, "City taken." The magistrates fined him for being verbose. "Taken," they said, would have sufficed.

The river of Athens is the Kephisos; the river in Sparta is the Eurotas. One time, an Athenian and a Spartan were trading insults.

> "We have buried many Spartans," said the
> Athenian, "beside the Kephisos." "Yes,"

replied the Spartan, "but we have buried no Athenians beside the Eurotas."

Another time, a band of Spartans arrived at a crossroads to find a party of frightened travelers. "You are lucky," the travelers told them. "A gang of bandits was here just a few minutes ago." "We were not lucky," said the Spartan leader. "They were."

In Sparta, the law was to keep everything simple. One ordinance decreed that you could not finish a roof beam with any tool finer than a hatchet. So all the roof beams in Sparta were basically logs.

> Once, a Spartan was visiting Athens and his host was showing off his own mansion, complete with finely detailed, square roof beams. The Spartan asked the Athenian if trees grew square in Athens. "No, of course not," said the Athenian, "but round, as trees grow everywhere." "And if they grew square," asked the Spartan, "would you make them round?"

Probably the most famous warrior quip of all is that of the

Spartan Dienekes at Thermopylae. When the Spartans first occupied the pass, they had yet to see the army of the Persian invaders. They had heard that it was big, but they had no idea how big.

> As the Spartans were preparing their defensive positions, a native of Trachis, the site of the pass, came racing into camp, out of breath and wide-eyed with terror. He had seen the Persian horde approaching. As the tiny contingent of defenders gathered around, the man declared that the Persian multitude was so numerous that, when their archers fired their volleys, the mass of arrows blocked out the sun.
>
> "Good," declared Dienekes. "Then we'll have our battle in the shade."

Several aspects of this quip—and Leonidas's remark about "sharing dinner in hell"—are worth noting.

First, they're not jokes. They're dead-on, but they're not delivered for laughs.

Second, they don't solve the problem. Neither remark offers

hope or promises a happy ending. They're not inspirational. The deliverers of these quips don't point to glory or triumph— or seek to allay their comrades' anxiety by holding out the prospect of some rosy outcome. The remarks confront reality. They say, "Some heavy shit is coming down, brothers, and we're going to go through it."

Lastly, these remarks are inclusive. They're about "us." Whatever ordeal is coming, the company will undergo it together. Leonidas's and Dienekes' quips draw the individual out of his private terror and yoke him to the group.

Even the epitaph of the Three Hundred (by the poet Simonides) is lean and terse. It leaves out almost every fact about the battle—the antagonists, the stakes, the event, the date, the war, the reason for it all. It assumes that the reader knows it all already and brings to it his own emotion.

> Go tell the Spartans, stranger passing by,
> that here, obedient to their laws, we lie.

The language of the Warrior Ethos is private. It speaks warrior to warrior and doesn't care if outsiders get it or not.

PART THREE

INNER WARS

21

CASUALTIES OF WAR

All of us know brothers and sisters who have fought with incredible courage on the battlefield, only to fall apart when they came home.

Why? Is it easier to be a soldier than to be a civilian?

For the warrior, all choices have consequences. His decisions have meaning; every act he takes is significant. What he says and does can save (or cost) his own life or the lives of his brothers. The nineteen-year-old squad leader and the twenty-three-year-old lieutenant often exercise more power (and in spheres of greater and more instant consequence) than their fathers, who are fifty and have been working honorably and diligently their entire lives.

Is adrenaline addictive? Is the fight? Are these tours of combat, hellish as they may feel in the moment, the best years of our lives?

22

THE CIVILIAN WORLD

Spartans and Romans and Macedonians, Persians and Mongols, Apache and Sioux, Masai and samurai and Pashtun all share one advantage over us Americans:

They were (and are) warrior cultures embedded within warrior societies.

This is not the case in the United States.

The American military is a warrior culture embedded within a civilian society.

This state is, in the American view, highly desirable. A too-strong military, unfettered by civilian restraint, might be inclined to adventurism or worse. No citizen disputes this or wishes to set things up any other way. The joint chiefs answer to Congress and to the president—and ultimately to the American people. This is the state that the Constitution intended and that the Founding Fathers, who were rightly wary of unchecked concentrations of power, had in mind.

But it is an interesting state—and one that produces curious effects.

First, the values of the warrior culture are not necessarily shared by the society at large. In fact, many of their values are opposites.

Civilian society prizes individual freedom. Each man and woman is at liberty to choose his or her own path, rise or fall, do whatever he or she wants, so long as it doesn't impinge on the liberty of others. The warrior culture, on the other hand, values cohesion and obedience. The soldier or sailor is not free to do whatever he wants. He serves; he is bound to perform his duty.

Civilian society rewards wealth and celebrity. Military culture prizes honor.

Aggression is valued in a warrior culture. In civilian life, you can go to jail for it.

A warrior culture trains for adversity. Luxury and ease are the goals advertised to the civilian world.

Sacrifice, particularly shared sacrifice, is considered an

71

opportunity for honor in a warrior culture. A civilian politician doesn't dare utter the word.

Selflessness is a virtue in a warrior culture. Civilian society gives lip service to this, while frequently acting as selfishly as it possibly can.

Is it healthy for a society to entrust its defense to one percent of its population, while the other 99 percent thanks its lucky stars that it doesn't have to do the dirty work?

In ancient Sparta and in the other cultures cited, a warrior culture (the army) existed within a warrior society (the community itself). No conflict existed between the two. Each supported and reinforced the other. Remember the stories about the Spartan mothers? When the Three Hundred were chosen to march out and die at Thermopylae, there was weeping and wailing in the streets of Sparta—by the wives and mothers of the warriors who were *not* chosen. The wives of the Three Hundred walked about dry-eyed and proud.

A hundred and fifty years later, Demosthenes, the great Athenian orator, delivered a series of speeches in the assembly on this very subject—willing sacrifice by all. The orations were called Philippics because they warned Athens against the rise of Philip of Macedonia, Alexander's father, whose ambition was clearly to bring all of Greece under his heel.

> Men of Athens, will you send your sons to contest this monster, Philip? Or have you grown so fat and happy that you care not, and dispatch instead hired troops, who are not of our blood or kin? Will these mercenaries, who fight only for profit, possess the will to hold Philip back? Or will the day come when we awake to discover that we have ceded future liberty to current ease?

The greatness of American society, like its Athenian progenitor, is that it is a civilian society. Freedom and equality are the engines that produce wealth, power, culture and art and unleash the greatness of the human spirit.

What is the place of the Warrior Ethos within a greater civilian society? That question has been asked from the days of the Minutemen through the World War II "Greatest Generation" to Vietnam and, today, to the conflicts in Iraq and Afghanistan.

The greatness of American society is that our citizens are still debating it—protected by those who have freely chosen to embrace the Warrior Ethos. And still debating it freely.

23

COMING HOME

But what about us? What about the soldier or Marine who steps off the plane from overseas and finds himself in the scariest place he's seen in years:

Home.

Has everything he knows suddenly become useless? What skill set can he employ in the civilian world? The returning warrior faces a dilemma not unlike that of the convict released from prison. Has he been away so long that he can never come back? Is the world he knows so alien to the "real world" that he can never fit in again?

Who is he, if he's not a warrior?

The answer may not be as far away as he supposes.

The returning warrior may not realize it, but he has acquired an MBA in enduring adversity and a Ph.D. in resourcefulness, tenacity and the capacity for hard work.

He may find that the warrior skills he has acquired are exactly what he and his family need. And more: that these skills possess the capacity to lift him and sustain him through the next stage of his life and through every succeeding stage.

The war remains the same. Only the field has changed.

The returning warrior possesses the Warrior Ethos, and this is a mighty ally in all spheres of endeavor.

24

"PURITY OF THE WEAPON"

The civilian sometimes misconstrues the warrior code; he takes it to be one of simple brutality. Overpower the enemy, show no mercy, win at all costs.

But the Warrior Ethos commands that brute aggression be tempered by self-restraint and guided by moral principle.

Soldiers of the Israeli Defense Forces (who often must fight against enemies who target civilians, who strike from or stockpile weapons within houses of worship and who employ their own women and children as human shields) are taught to act according to a principle called *Tohar HaNeshek:* "purity of the weapon." This derives from two verses in the Old Testament. What it means is that the individual soldier must reckon, himself, what is the moral use of his weapon and what is the immoral use.

When an action is unjust, the warrior must not take it.

Alexander, in his campaigns, always looked beyond the

immediate clash to the prospect of making today's foe into tomorrow's ally. After conquering an enemy in the field, his first act was to honor the courage and sacrifice of his antagonists—and to offer the vanquished warriors a place of honor within his own corps. By the time Alexander reached India, his army had more fighters from the ranks of his former enemies than from those of his own Greeks and Macedonians.

Cyrus of Persia believed that the spoils of his victories were meant for one purpose—so that he could surpass his enemies in generosity.

> I contend against my foes in this arena only: the capacity to be of greater service to them than they are to me.

Alexander operated by the same principle.

> Let us conduct ourselves so that all men wish to be our friends and all fear to be our enemies.

The capacity for empathy and self-restraint will serve us powerfully, not only in our external wars but in the conflicts within our own hearts.

25

THE WAR INSIDE OURSELVES

The *Bhagavad-Gita* is the great warrior epic of India. For thousands of years, Indian caste structure has been dominated by two elite social orders—the Brahmins (poets and holy men) and the Kshatriyas (warriors and nobles). The *Bhagavad-Gita* is the story of the great warrior Arjuna, who receives spiritual instruction from his charioteer, who happens to be Krishna—i.e., God in human form.

Krishna instructs Arjuna to slay his enemies without mercy. The warrior-god points across the battlefield to knights and archers and spearmen whom Arjuna knows personally and feels deep affection for—and commands him to kill them all. But here's the interesting part:

The names of these enemy warriors, in Sanskrit, can be read two ways. They can be simply names. Or they can represent inner crimes or personal vices, such as greed, jealousy, selfishness, the capacity to play our friends false or to act without compassion toward those who love us.

In other words, our warrior Arjuna is being instructed to slay the enemies *inside himself.*

Human history, anthropologists say, can be divided into three stages—savagery, barbarism and civilization. Warrior codes arose during the period known as High Barbarism. Many noble cultures fall under this category, from Native American tribes to Cyrus's Persians to the Greeks and Trojans made immortal in Homer's *Iliad*. The Warrior Ethos's origins are primitive. Its genesis lies in the eye-for-an-eye ethic of humanity's most ancient and primordial epochs.

The *Bhagavad-Gita* changes this. It takes the Warrior Ethos and elevates it to a loftier and nobler plane—the plane of the individual's inner life, to his struggle to align himself with his own higher nature.

26

THE LORD OF DISCIPLINE

In the *Gita*, the warrior Arjuna is commanded to slay the "foes" that constitute his own baser being. That is, to eradicate those vices and inner demons that would sabotage his path to becoming his best and highest self.

How is Arjuna instructed to do this? By the practice of self-discipline. In other words, by the interior exercise of his exterior Warrior Ethos.

Arjuna's divine instructor (one of whose titles in Sanskrit is "Lord of Discipline") charges his disciple to:

> Fix your mind upon its object.
> Hold to this, unswerving,
> Disowning fear and hope,
> Advance only upon this goal.

Here is the Warrior Ethos directed inward, employing the same virtues used to overcome external enemies—but enlisting these qualities now in the cause of the inner struggle for integrity, maturity and the honorable life.

27

A RITE OF PASSAGE

Why do young men and women in a free society enlist in the military? The act seems to defy common sense. Why volunteer for low pay, lame haircuts and the chance to be killed—particularly in a society that rewards such behavior with little of more substance than a "Thank you for your service" or a yellow ribbon on a bumper sticker? Why do it? Why sign up?

One answer may be that the young man or woman is seeking a rite of passage.

When we enlist in the Army or the Marine Corps, we're looking for a passage to manhood or womanhood. We have examined our lives in the civilian world and concluded, perhaps, that something's missing. Do we lack self-discipline? Self-confidence? Do we feel stuck? Are we heading in the right direction?

We want action. We seek to test ourselves. We want friends—real friends, who will put themselves on the line for us—and we want to do the same for them. We're seeking some force that will hurl us out of our going-nowhere lives and into the real world, into genuine hazard and risk. We want to be part of something greater than ourselves, something we can be proud of. And we want to come out of the process as different (and better) people than we were when we went in. We want to be men, not boys. We want to be women, not girls.

We want a rite of passage. We want to grow up.

One way to do that is to go to war. Young men have been undergoing that ordeal of initiation for ten thousand years. This passage is into and through what the great psychologist Carl Jung called "the Warrior Archetype."

28

THE WARRIOR ARCHETYPE

Jung was a student of myths and legend and of the unconscious. He discovered and named the Collective Unconscious, meaning that part of the psyche that is common to all cultures in all eras and at all times.

The Collective Unconscious, Jung said, contains the stored wisdom of the human race, accumulated over thousands of generations.

The Collective Unconscious is the software we're born with. It's our package of instincts and preverbal knowledge. Within this package, Jung discovered what he called the archetypes.

Archetypes are the larger-than-life, mythic-scale personifications of the stages that we pass through as we mature. The youth, the lover, the wanderer, the joker, the king or queen, the wise man, the mystic. Legendary tales like that of King Arthur and the Knights of the Round Table are populated by archetypes. Movies are full of archetypes. Even a deck of cards has archetypes: king, queen, joker, jack.

Archetypes serve the purpose of guiding us as we grow. A new archetype kicks in at each stage. It makes the new phase "feel right" and "seem natural."

One of the primary archetypes is the Warrior. The warrior archetype exists across all eras and nations and is virtually identical in every culture.

In their book *King, Warrior, Magician, Lover,* authors Robert Moore and Douglas Gillette tell us that the human individual matures *from archetype to archetype.* A boy, for instance, evolves sequentially through the youth, the wanderer, the lover, the warrior, through husband and father to teacher, king, sage and mystic.

The warrior archetype clicks in like a biological clock sometime in the early to mid-teens. We join a gang, we try out for the football team, we hang with our homies, we drive fast, we take crazy chances, we seek adventure and hazard. That'll change later. When the husband/father archetype kicks in, we'll trade in our 500-horsepower Mustang and buy a Prius. But not yet.

For now, the warrior archetype has seized us. Something inside us makes us want to jump out of airplanes and blow stuff up. Something makes us seek out mentors—tough old sergeants to put us through hell, to push us past our limits, to find out what we're capable of. And we seek out comrades in arms. Brothers who will get our backs and we'll get theirs, lifelong friends who are just as crazy as we are.

29

THE NAKED WISE MEN

Moore and Gillette say something further. They state that the experiences and wisdom we accumulate under one archetype become the foundation for all the succeeding archetypes.

In other words, the lessons we learn are not wasted. The virtues we acquire during our time in the warrior archetype we can use when we mature into the husband and father, the mentor, the king. We get to keep them—and profit from them—our whole lives.

> Alexander in India encountered some gymnosophist (literally "naked wise men") yogis, sitting in meditation in the sun on the banks of the Indus. Alexander's party was trying to get through the busy street, but the yogis had their spot and they wouldn't move. One of Alexander's zealous young lieutenants took it upon himself to chase the holy men out of the king's path. When one of the wise

men resisted, the officer started verbally abusing him. Just then, Alexander came up. The lieutenant pointed to Alexander and said to the yogi, "This man has conquered the world! What have you accomplished?" The yogi looked up calmly and replied, "I have conquered the need to conquer the world."

At this, Alexander laughed with approval. He admired the naked wise men. "Could I be any man in the world other than myself," he said, "I would be this man here."

What Alexander was acknowledging was that the yogi was a warrior too. An inner warrior. Alexander looked at him and thought, "This man was a fighter when he was my age. He has taken the lessons he learned as a warrior dueling external enemies and is turning them to use now as he fights internal foes to achieve mastery over himself."

30

THE HARDEST THING
IN THE WORLD

The hardest thing in the world is to be ourselves.

Who are we? Our family tells us, society tells us, laws and customs tell us. But what do *we* say? How do we get to that place of self-knowledge and conviction where we are able to state without doubt, fear or anger, "This is who I am, this is what I believe, this is how I intend to live my life"?

How do we find our true calling, our soul companions, our destiny?

In this task, our mightiest ally is the Warrior Ethos.

Directed inward, the Warrior Ethos grounds us, fortifies us and focuses our resolve.

As soldiers, we have been taught discipline. Now we teach ourselves self-discipline.

As fighting men and women, we have been motivated, commanded and validated by others. Now we school ourselves in self-motivation, self-command, self-validation.

The Warrior Archetype is not the be-all and end-all of life. It is only one identity, one stage on the path to maturity. But it is the greatest stage—and the most powerful. It is the foundation upon which all succeeding stages are laid.

Let us be, then, warriors of the heart, and enlist in our inner cause the virtues we have acquired through blood and sweat in the sphere of conflict—courage, patience, selflessness, loyalty, fidelity, self-command, respect for elders, love of our comrades (and of the enemy), perseverance, cheerfulness in adversity and a sense of humor, however terse or dark.

BIBLIOGRAPHY

The stories and anecdotes in this book come from the following sources (though the author admits he sometimes can't remember which came from where). All citations are translations or reconstructions by the author.

Arrian, *The Campaigns of Alexander*

Bhagavad-Gita, numerous translations

Curtius, *History of Alexander*

Demosthenes, *Philippics*

Frontinus, *Stratagemata*

Herodotus, *The Histories*

Homer, *Iliad*

Moore, Robert and Douglas Gillette, *King Warrior Magician Lover: Rediscovering the Archetypes of the Mature Masculine*

Plutarch, *Moralia* (including *Sayings of the Spartans* and *Sayings of the Spartan Women*)

Plutarch, *Life of Lycurgus*

Plutarch, *Life of Alexander*

Plutarch, *Life of Epaminondas*

Polyaenus, *Stratagemata*

Thucydides, *History of the Peloponnesian War*

Vegetius, *De Re Militari*

Xenophon, *Constitution of the Spartans*

Xenophon, *The Education of Cyrus*

Xenophon, *Anabasis* ["The March Upcountry"]

STEVEN PRESSFIELD is the author of *Gates of Fire*, *Tides of War*, *The Afghan Campaign* and *Killing Rommel*, among others. He is a former Marine. In 2003, he was made an honorary citizen by the city of Sparta in Greece.